Memories of days which we live

Mark Robins

BookLeaf Publishing

India | USA | LK

Presentation by *BookLeaf Publishing*

Web: www.bookleafpub.com

E-mail: info@bookleafpub.com

ISBN:9789358317381

First edition 2023

DEDICATION

You all are important to the creation of my life in being a creative spark in seeing me grow.

Without you, my life would be different and whom knows not writing this book of 21 days in my life whom the dedication is too.

ACKNOWLEDGEMENT

To Christine Louie for my creativity and Tony
(Frank Anthony) for my tenacity, to Darren,
Andrew & Teresa (Terri, which she prefers) for
being there in moments of my life when I
needed them most, to Kaye my partner and
Elaine and Sylv who are long life friends with
the sincerity and wisdom whom are integral to
my life.

Also, great friends such as Lisa and her partner
Megan, Andrea & Heidi to name a few to my
family in America gives me strength to shine
through.

Each of whom need acknowledgement and in a
small way that I show, these memories of my
life are lived all through you.

PREFACE

These words of the heart are written with affection and respect for the ones whom make me happy and for those whom have given me strength to carry on.

From family to great friends and loved ones as well as partner included, to list them all a book in itself would need to be written.

A bacon sandwich on a Sunday morning.

A bacon sandwich on a Sunday morning.

As I wake up this morning , with sleepiness in
my eyes, the smell of the morning tells me
enough of bye byes.

The television in the background, playing music
of the sixties to gently stimulate the mind to one
of life's fixes.

A strong black decaffeinated coffee awakens the
mind, soul and body to tell myself that I'm
living with another body.

From music of the sixties to trucking hell, a
hunger comes over me that won't rid me of a
smell.

I know that it may be simple but the cleanup of
such a simple piece of meat, gives the craving it
demands in my heart, mind and body In
relishing it's treat.

The bread is toasting as the bacon is lightly fried
with white pudding cooked and butter slides,
with some brown sauce and some spice a
creation is made to look pleasing to the eyes,
down to the stomach it glides.

The memories of cleaning still linger in the
distance but the enjoyment of a sandwich
compels no rush of me to be wincing.

As it is Sunday after all, a day to be relaxed in
watching some tv and a toasted bacon sandwich
in awe, with a plate showing stains of what was
just consumed, to be relaxed after all and in self
be amused.

Life's pleasures are sweet no matter how small,
by recognising these pleasures we all can be free
from life's stresses and worries within one and
all.

A meeting with management of grievance.

Today, I awoke wondering what order things
should be done, a meeting at 1 to vent my
grievance bar none.

So, as I saw with eyes the dreary weather came
through French doors, with a morning coffee,
put away the crocks, to having a shower I adore.

The place now tidy and an espresso with
shredded wheat for breakfast and uniformed
tidied to look as business should be.

Next, photocopying letters and documents to
give, as a representation of my grievance I live.

Many pages are there like a short War & Peace,
in detailing the obvious of time conflicts and
beast.

These pages extend the beginning as though,
nothing untoward to begin unraveling a tale of
woe.

As the pages are read, the rest starts to unfold,
that leads the recipient of more that needs to be
told.

With these pages printing in the background, the
cartridge runs out of ink, as NCIS on the tv, the
black and white page becomes a slight shade of
green to yellow link.

These pages continue as there is more to be said
in completing a grievance of an unjust toward.

36 pages printed now, reads like a short novel
that only seems like doom as the rest continues
to unravel.

The point of all this, leads to determination and
understanding, that fighting for your right to live
takes an amount of not bystanding.

Be positive and courageous as life deals you
battles, to now that you've done your best in
being somebody.

As the majority of persons are now just a
number whom can be, replaced by the flick of an
electronic eraser.

We are all individuals, unique and must stand up
to oppression, otherwise we will never be
recognised by pure aggression.

So, my meeting this afternoon, I will go
prepared and determined, to express my
grievance at their inactions.

My job I enjoy, giving positivity and joy, to all
I'm welcome of our journey of discovery.

The meeting today, was pleasant and jovial to
give me a radiance of which I'm now flowing.

That I've been listened and understood to the
past two months of emotions, which have been a
rollercoaster of a ride that have had no devotion.

I feel enthusiastic to my future a positive
outcome my way, that in my persevering
tenacity shall prevent others feeling this pain.

It's 8:06 in the morning, 11 degrees with Autumn in the air.

I've woken up early with the start of a cold in my body, the head is buzzing and my nose runny.

I'm lay on a sofa with a sleeping bag snuggling, to keep the cold air that's rustling through the door ajar bugling.

The fresh air a cleansing, to be rid of the bugs, in preparation of my weekend of a men's stag do weekend.

In order to heal, the body needs to rest, with a decaffeinated tea and a cold slice of pizza, to give body some fuel for pizzazz.

The sky is bright blue without a cloud nearby, the trees are as still and nobody passing by.

The leaves are turning from green to an auburn brown, as the autumn slumbers into winter with our faces beginning to frown.

The days are now getting colder after a summer
with heat and frivolity for us to wear more to
keep us warmer from hostilities.

The snow will be with us at sometime in the
year, to lower the temperature to wish back for
cheer.

To then look forward to the new year and the
warm weather which follows with parties of
beer.

So as I rest, now 8:25 in the morning, Simon
Templar The Saint, saves a life from another
person mourning.

A chest feeling wheezy as the cold takes a hold
of my body at 11 degrees on this Tuesday
morning.

A hot toddy I'm thinking with fresh lemon and
whiskey to be rid of this cold, so, for a Stag Do
in Blackpool be frisky.

Life's little annoyances, having a cold on a cold
day can be generally a seasonal thing, but
unfortunately not for me.

As I've lived with them all my life and that's the
way it shall be, at 8:06 in the morning, 11
degrees on an Autumn day.

Teatime with a homemade Turkey mince & Chicken Jalfrezi Lasagne.

On a cool night in the Autumn's breeze, a meal fulfilling which should be a breeze, already prepped on Sunday I did, with other assortments in batch cooking to enjoy with a variety indeed.

Last night it was, homemade chicken & potato curry with rice that burst with flavours and punch, to be rid of a flu which is haunting my weekend that could be hot and frisky at lunch.

The meals I cook, are natural and filling to fill not only the eyes but also the stomach as the colder days draw nearer in a mobile home I live, living on food with such flavours can be tricky but neat.

So, tonight was a Lasagna of my own concoctions and taste, by using what's left in the freezer and cupboards to bake the chicken was seasoned with salt and Cajun spice, the Turkey mince and pickles to be layered with bechamel and jalfrezi sauce.

The aromas spread around with garlic bread in
the air and baby potatoes, sweetcorn, broccoli
and cauliflower to compliment, as the food went
down well, a sense of heat from the jalfrezi, to
fill up soul and stomach on a cool Autumn's eve.

A meal prepared with love, is a wonderful time,
when spent with a person whom is amazed at my
concoctions with a plate clean and spotless, to
say is there some more, yes there is but not
tonight.

A home, no matter the size or type gives love
when food is in the air, to those whom
appreciate and enjoy the flavours they're given
with love.

Life's river of voyage on the cruise ship of life.

To the future we have in-front of us as we leave the past behind, our memories of the doors we've opened and heard the voices of our decisions echo in our shadows, we embark on the sways of the seas to the mysteries of flow from the undercurrents which could steer us off course to an island of magical mystery and wonder in where we make new friends by challenging the beginnings of what is yet to happen.

These travels are termed to some as destiny, whereas to other, it's just circumstances of opportunity, either way, embrace the future, keep the past to be remembered if need be, love life each day as the sunrises from the horizon that life is a marvel to be be explored in the mysteries of the universe before our feet, bodies, heart and mind to be the tapestry of our lives.

As the movement of the seas is ever changing, so is the course of our destiny with the undercurrents wanting to pull us under but our determination to keep us on a steady course to the destination we see in our minds.

Morning towards Blackpool.
(Part 1/3)

The day is bright with birds singing in the trees, on my way to collect others for a stag do 4 hours' drive away, arriving on their doorstep, most of whom I've never met, shaking hands and pleasantries with fun in their minds I bet.

Drinking and eating as well as some betting I fear to a night of funny walking due to the brew that will be consumed, once in Blackpool, the bags are dropped in the room, down to the bar in motel as the drinking consumed, to then say the first nights events will be starting in a few hours' time.

A pub crawl treasure hunt that is digitally found by using a mobile phone, but the drinking is real, a Guinness I chose, and then one after the other with beers and shots, all ring out as the cash machine rings "Ching Ching".

A walk along the promenade to find the clues and some laughter along the way to eventually find that the treasure hunt has now become just a pub crawl, Blackpool's light's guide the road for

"

travellers and participants as the food stalls waft
their luring scent to be tempted after drinking
alcohol all night.
Eventually its 4am the following morn to know
that another day of events will start, but how
many will be up, I know that I'm 1. I can't
guarantee the other 5 but will see.

I go for breakfast and to my surprise, there be???

Activities at Blackpool (Part 2/3)

All 6 of us are up, only one couldn't stomach breakfast, so onto the next day's events, Go-Karting, which should be fun, 5 boozed up fiends and one whom is sober, whom do you think will be the winner?
We sign the waiver and then get shown the course, get suited up in overalls and wear head gear, few rounds to settle in, before let loose on our own, completing as many laps our bodies will endure.

Round and round we go which seems never ending, spinning into the tyres sometimes, but the more and more you push the feeling is so exhilarating, as we pass one another, the time is lost into the ether of the moment which then comes to the finale and find out who the winner was.

The one who couldn't eat breakfast was the winner whereas the one who was sober, came in last, go figure.
as we all am live our lives in Blackpool someday somewhere.

Later that day, to a football match we went that
ended in 4-1 result to the delight of the stag, as
was his team playing in Blackpool, fortunately
the weather was warm but no need for a pool.

We then headed back to hotel where I decided to
rest for the following day's journey home which
I thought was best, the lads went to their last
event which was a flop that should've been the
highlight of their night but more consuming of
beverages were had that they could've sunk a
battleship as I witnessed there intoxication first
hand.

Off to bed they went as I was getting ready for
the new day in hand, they sore heads me buzzing
like a bird in a tree, a blinder is all I can say but
who am I to judge.

Travelling home from Blackpool (Part 3/3)

So, now the frivolities end and the stomachs are full with booze and food with our pockets emptied of the spending fortune upon we took.

Scoot around the room to see if any underwear lurking that shouldn't be, to sealing the bags before handing the key, load up the minibus and breakfast is waiting before onto the promenade once more, gifts and souvenirs, sticks of rock as well as fridge magnets to please.

Now all loaded and on our way home, four hours again along the motorways twisting lengths to awaiting arms of those once left behind, the weekend gone in a blink as though just a sliver of smashed glass twinkling in the sun, the memories of the sands with the coast gently swirling over the top giving memories once more.

Finally arrived home safely, with faces beaming to see the loved ones back once more but for me still more to be done, as one final trip to my home before I can say I'm done, my partner waiting patiently whilst she has been alone these past few days wishing I was by her side, the place that feels safe and warm is where the heart knows best.

A trip of expectancies I wasn't surprised but memories I may not want to experience again as a Stag do is a wild beast when not tamed, so have fun and don't be shy as all whom are there to let their hair down too.

Life is to be lived even if it's just enjoying a stag do with friends.

A Monday same as the rest follows as the weeks merge into one.

A coffee stirs the brain cells as there are echoes
in the background, my partner gone to work
early as I rest in my gown, the day after the
weekend before, stiff and aching from the events
of frivolity to consider running a bath or let the
shower wash away the festivities.

The hours begin to mount as the sunshine
radiates through the door, I get up and return the
hired vehicle to its port then upon returning
home I strive for a sandwich but the roads take
me on a different journey, I go to a greasy Joes.

A baguette as long as my forearm, filled with
sausage, bacon, mushrooms, eggs and sauce that
my eyes begin to wonder if I should have over
the next two days.

A message to a friend and he replies "Fancy a
ride?", so a bacon and sausage bap I purchase
for him, meet up where his next break be, to chat

and laugh over the size of my baguette, then
depart our separate ways.

We then meet later for a coffee and a chat, some
heartfelt things revealed that show an insight
never seen, the demons we carry can be a
daunting thing, so having a friend without
judgement is a treasured thing.

Hours have passed on, now time to mosey on
with reassurance words in saying that I'm here,
appreciative and understood we bring, our
Mondays can be mundane but we can change the
norm in being a great friend by not allowing
them to merge into one.

Be the difference and you'll see the importance
of whom we all are.

Tuesday, a day of uncertainties

Kaye returns from work 2 hours early, in severe stiffness and pain which is hard to see, I get her to rest on the sofa whilst I put the kettle in, hot water bottle to the ready and two tea towels to wrap, so that the heat gently oozes through to give her some relief.

A bath I run, with just hot water and I then ask her come to the bathroom in which she slowly aches her way, getting in with no need for cool Runnings as her body slowly eases into the salted bath water.

A sigh of gentle relief as the warmth radiates through, there half an hour to then eventually leave the baths warming caress onwards to a warm soothing bed that cradles her aching body as the continual warming hot bottle pinpoints directly to her pain.

5 hours pass, sleeping through her pain, at ease and loved, wakens to needing sustenance which is filling and nutritious to then back to bed allowing the nurturing care to continually heal

the fragility of life which was in so much
discomfort early that afternoon.

By the following morning dawn, those memories
of the day past are still lingering but less angst
within the body to say, "Thank you for listening
and allowing me to heal through rest. You are
my only body and I worship the love you are
giving me".

We all have to listen to our bodies in being
respectful, so that we can continue to live but
even if we are not able to give what our bodies
need every day, showing that we care is a great
start to being there in the days that we are
privileged to share and live with others.

Wednesday, shopping to the max

A chore of our daily lives which can be rewarding but also takes time when unloading from the car, you think that not much is bought, until you unpack, those empty compartments in the cupboard and fridge before long become full bursting to the seam as if to say "Dream on".

So a game of Tetris so to speak as I continue to see 4 more bags on the floor to unpack and think to myself "A coffee I need", 5 minutes breather and the onslaught again begins, thinking, "I'm sure there wasn't that much left", so onwards I go and the last bag is eventually reached to stand back and admired the craftsmanship of what has been achieved.

£300.00 spent and now not hungry, but a chicken left to defrost to cook tomorrow, so now it is seasoned and put into a dish, to suddenly realise "Where the hell is that going to go in the fridge to season over night - aaaaarrrrgghhh".

So once more, some more reorganising and once again by some magnitude, the fridge is bursting at the seams, screaming as if to say, "Greed is a sin so why are you forcing it onto me?"

A fiery pot noodle is all I can manage now as the efforts expelled leave me too shattered to cook, the kettle switched on and the foil lid peeled away, sachets of seasoning opened and hey presto, a hot meal in 5.

TV on with Law & Order - Special Victims in the background, twirling the fork into the noodles and speaking to partner on WhatsApp is a well-deserved break after shopping to the max on a Wednesday noon.

Who ever said that retail therapy was relaxing is a person who goes shopping but has the hard work done for them because for me, from the time I started to the moment I sat down with noodles, my therapy started in putting my feet up.

We all have busy lives, so take time and enjoy the finer retail therapies, so let others once in a while help you get your happy retail therapy done and go for a meal at a pub and let the fridge breathe a sigh of relief.

Thursday a visit to Nuffield orthopaedic

Today I went to the hospital to see my partner Kaye, before she went into surgery and there she lay, in a gown unflattering to all but kept her dignity in the bed for nurses to call, the usual checks they do in a room white and bright with ITV in the background shedding some insight to knowledge which bores to the mobile for a byte or two.

Her face brightens the room as to say to the sun shining through, "Don't steal my limelight as I'm the one in hospital with my man come to visit me, you've had your time guiding him here, now go and find someone else for the moment to shine".

The corridors so colourful and the personalities fill the place which brings fear and dread to ease the visitors that they themselves feel at peace to give reassurance to those who'd elsewhere prefer to be.

So as I give her the overnight bag, out pops her Rock Ape, a snuggle buddy whom has been with

her through thick and thin to say, "I'm here to
give you a cuddle and kiss" until the day she
returns to my side, cheeky character who wears
a hoody and has a big clock on a chain round his
neck but loves bananas morning, noon and night.

The operation went as proposed but more days
are required to be in the hospital bed, so drab
meals and bed rest are the orders of the specialist
with checks throughout the day to be a reminder
that the nurses are caring in the right way.

Their charm and charisma to help you feel loved
and cared for in getting you home, but not until
they are safe in the knowledge that you won't be
alone, a duty they learnt to cherish from the
onset of their training to the days onward in
being on a ward by your bed.

They answer questions if they know or get the
one whom will give you an understanding if
unsure, a doctor, nurse, specialist, anaesthetist,
therapist, security officer to an administrative
assistant are all significant in getting help and
reassurance to my loved one health be as best it
can be.

My partner is a person important to me and
whom Rock Ape loves, that is why we are

privileged and honoured to have such caring and
wonderful professionals to give care we cherish,
I am forever in awe of the role you are in our
lives and showing that respect can be given with
love and honesty, no matter our divides as we
are all human living a life on this one planet in
which we all share forevermore.
Thank you.   Mark X.

Friday, catching up on poems.

The intellectual chat of others confine us to
needing technologies which encompass our days
in getting done by conversing our emotions for
others hearing words written by someone else.

My TV was showing old programmes as I woke
up, to then listen to music from yesteryear and
beyond for many hours whilst posting my
writings, Dr Hook "When you in love with a
beautiful woman" to Celine Dion "I'm Alive" to
ABBA and more.

Technology has an incremental part in being
glued to our fingers with our gaze upon a screen
instead should be looking at the world in front of
our eyes to see the potential of life utilising all
of our senses together.

The challenges of life are a constant moving
tangible part in which we decide how we
progress and what we choose to experience
without technology, it's now 13:45, I have been
sat in this one place since 07:45 talking, writing,
listening, conceptualising but still motionless

apart from my fingers on a computer no bigger than a remote.

When life calls up on you as in the words of Celine Dion "When you call on me ………….. I'm Alive" is truly saying that there is more to life through friendship and integration without the need of technology being an integral part of our time.

We all have someone whom we can call upon by taking the risk of putting the mobile in its place of authority and state "I'm in control of my life, not you, you technical masterpiece of wizardry that draws me to a flame like a moth seeing beauty in what's seen but ignoring the dangers".

Put the mobile down and be in touch with human reality instead of Artificial Intelligence once in a while and memories will be forever a part in our minds instead of being in our phones, my daily poems are written and posted which took most of the day but I'm at fault, no one else and lost the beauty which was there for me to be seen instead through a piece of glass.

So, now to be more productive and move from my shaped curvature sofa position to a more

positive action this afternoon in which the day is
then not lost.

Saturday. The eve of my birthday

A day which I've forgotten about, to Thatcham I should've went, to see some friends representing Pride, my apologies I sent, as all the time passed was too late for me to travel, so I went to see my partner sooner, in hospital I decided my presence should be.

Her eyes lit up like stars in the night as I explained my decision to see her sooner and a glimmer of laughter from her lips as I explained my frivolities to her, the day was taken by surprise which was cause for my forgetfulness that the ladies whom I was going to meet up, made a comment "A birthday cake I would get" if I turned up a day later.

So, the rest of the eve I talked and talked till the cows jumped over the moon till the early hours of the following morn, did a welcoming visit come and he felt the earth move as did the cows and the moon.

Our days are eventful if we let ourselves be free to enjoy the bounties before us, by being true to

natures and glowing in-front of others, we all
have opportunities to make happiness whilst free
and balance the good in life with reflections
aplenty.

Sunday, 55 Today is the year 1968

The day on which I celebrate 55 times in my life is a milestone of remembrance to my advancement in becoming me, we have turmoil's many as well as happy to be photographed for reflection to show our families and friends in years to come.

The day is sunny and the roof down driving to meet friends at Thatcham on their campaign, to others understanding of Pride on life and its importance of being nice, a lunchtime meal as well as a drink, leads to a lengthy conversation with Andrea, politics and differences which divide the world into conflicts and wars instead of happiness and peace.

From there, on my way to see Kaye, a message from my brother second to me, wishing me blessings on my day to conflict of our own and anger it pursues, the anger, my partner sees of which support and understanding is given that fall into the night with the pain which now lessens to be a distant memory.

A meet from a new friend takes the night still to
some frustration but lingering anger must be
holding onto emotions which can't be hidden or
taken from me, so goodnight to my partner then
to bed eventually I go, into deep slumber with a
machine and no longer my worries I show.

The intricacies of life will always be moving
sometimes hard to follow, so hold on to the good
and let the bad ease to live a life of peace &
happiness.

Monday, Frustrations and hostilities

The day after my birthday on which I was born, 55 years ago I was just a small treasure to my mother whom the first to start a family of what I'm not knowing, my years of forming my personality were hindered by my father, to be a shy and not assertive participant in life's magical tapestry.

Off to school we went and homework was done with chores along the days that gave us much more to whom we were to become, those days of our youths were insignificant at that time but are now the basis of myself to this day.

Upon the day which gave me a choice was my grandparents on my mother's side, took myself and my two brothers in from the horrors which ripped through our lives, we were broken and split from a life which had been controlled, to ensure that the focus of family life was nothing more than a tool.

To grow up as children wasn't our choice in life, as we weren't the first choice of our father

mostly nor so I understand our mother, if a
daughter was born first, then maybe no more
would've followed as which 3 sons and then a
daughter gave cause for resentment.

To this day, 55 years on, no understanding do I
have as to the way I was treated including to
remember it's all locked away, but we live our
life by choices and whom I am today I can say I
am proud, as I am strong from those lessons on
which I've been formed.

Many souls are broken by the cruelties of family
horrors and unfairness, sometimes one person
does their best to give light and reassurance that
all will be bright, for me that will be my sister as
her resilience and strength outshines the
darkness in which we all lived to say we will
have our days.

We still fight and argue but that's part of
family's nature to be disagreeing as we continue
on life's majestic journey and discovery into our
hearts and minds of whom we become, In the
days and years to follow, our loved ones be, by
our side no more, enjoy all of whom they be
even if you don't agree

Tuesday, Light & Darkness is the order of the day.

A day of fun with a tinge of darkness, the morning of personalities intertwine with the meeting of new friends, to enjoy the freedom of choice as the day progresses to the realisation of sadness, we within the confines of our bodies through the day have to make decisions for the responsibilities to be safe and secure whilst enjoying our futures.

So a catch-up with my partner whom herself is resting in hospital, is listening to my news of the events which in the past have now a reflection of the future, the hours I spend with her today are a measure in which are cherished, as to bringing closer the days where she is back by my side to continue her healing at home.

Being positive in the steps that follow to bring harmony and a balance to our life whilst awaiting for the darkness of the day to pass, has been informing others of my decision to distance myself temporarily but enforcing that safety is paramount for all.

So, productive gains at the end of the evening
lead to an eventful end of the day and let my
body relax for the morn to follow in reviving a
body for a more fulfilling future to prosper in, a
final call of the evening to my partner via
WhatsApp will give her reassurance that I am
happy as much as can be and one day soon she
will be by side once more.

All leading to happiness and self-assurance that
they too will lead their future in being
responsible for others future.

Wednesday is the day that life becomes brighter.

In the days we live, there are choices to make an impact on our futures as well as others, we can either to decide to participate and accept the fate or see the fate of our inactions materialise to a possibility which could've been avoided.

Whether to have a chip butty and a battered sausage for lunch or a salad and bottle of water, walk to the appointment which is 10 minutes each way or be lazy and use the car, I'll have the chip buttie and battered sausage as I can then get some exercise to walk off the stodge I've consumed.

As I'm writing this for my appointment at the clinic, Peter Cetera is singing "Glory of Love" from The Karate Kid to suggest to me that life is to be lived with those whom make you happy, at the other clinic, is my partner waiting to be collected to take her home after being in hospital since last week waiting for her "Glory of Love".

We all search for happiness in this spectrum of time and hope that we live a life of fulfilment to

our last days on the coil of life, continually in
life, we are given challenges and opportunities
which give us choices to steer our decisions
from thoughts that give us happiness.

If not so, then we are the ones to change so that
we can see the future forward and let others see
our happiness which will bring them happiness
too, so be respectful, kind, true and pure hearted
as life will be a true friend if you allow it to be.

Thursday is a day of reflection with Kaye

Her first morning home instead of the hospital in
which she lay, a peaceful contented look upon
her face I see, as I go about making her
comfortable to the days chores still to be more.

Her car still at the hospital, Kaye not allowed to
drive with her foot bandaged, so on the bus I
travel and chat to colleagues with a hot latte in
hand scolding me as the bumps almost causing
foe me to need bandaging.

Eventually, I arrive at Nuffield hospital to search
for her car which starts at first turn of the key, to
telephone her and say that I'm on my way, the
windows open as the smell of old cigarettes in
the fabric cling to my chest, I say to Kaye how
did she get the car into such a state when she
only cleaned it recently.

Eventually, I parked her car safely to then
embark on a journey again to collect my car no
so far, to arrive home and realise I should've
have gone shopping first for some milk and bits.

A chicken roast I prepared for the evening meal
to suddenly remember the forgotten items that
were meant to be, so tidied up the crocks from
tea and then back out to Asda for me, II decided
to shop by Scan and go to the machine say "A
random security item check was needed", so a
store colleague I found and a look of frustration
upon her face but when she asked that she nulls
transaction and scans through again, I said "Yes
please".

Once completed, the bill I paid, before she left, I
asked "Can I go around again" with a cheeky
grin to which she replied "NO!!" with some
authority but a happy wink, just by the smallest
of gestures, a warm considering heart and mind,
we can brighten a person's evening as they come
to the end of their day and see that life is fine.

Friday close to the weekend and finish line in sight.

A busy day has started with sorting out the laundry to making a chicken & vegetable soup to cleaning the bathroom and an interesting conversation with a specialist, in the back of my mind, my 21 day challenge coming to a close, rereading the errors to make more sense to me. So many errors but time well spent to ensure a story I'm telling.

It first started as just a reflection of my personality to being more personal upon which I intended, trials and tribulations to fun times with whom I love, shows that our days are each unique, we forget to see those whom surround our life which in the complexities of life go so fast that we rarely show or see the impact of actions that make life so important.

Just a quick joke to the words "I Love you" are as important as being present and listening to a friend whom has worries on their mind.

We approach each day, hopefully with a vigour of fortitude to live every moment that we are

privileged as in one moment, we could be taken
from our choice to live and no longer our actions
become continually prominent, in memories of
others we then become or could be the other way
round that the missing begins and the chances of
choices cease to be in that moment.

Our lives are a moment of action to give others
some moments to cherish forevermore and
remember that we were unique because of whom
we are and we're, never to be taken for granted
as in that moment they may never be there
again.

So these words which have been written are a
momentum of my life as a picture on a mobile,
to be enjoyed as I'm here now sharing my love
for life, so cherish me now, never to taken
granted for as I share my life.

Reflection of 21 days writing

The life in which we live can be as mysterious and unique as the mammals and phylum, who we cohabit our lives with, from the Egyptian cats that walk with an air of regency to the hyenas whom laugh consistently there are jellyfish that glow beauty and finesse to hid a deadly secret beneath their flesh.

We have dogs whom treat us as Lord and Master to us dressing them to like a disaster, but no matter how we live our lives, we do so free from hatred as the future of our children brought an unsuspecting undercurrents of time which move against the fragility.

Times are a changing as we have Pride awareness around the world with labels being personalised to their own personalities. The age of coercion where we listened to our elders has now become the age of our youngsters bringing phoenix's from the ashes.

No matter our colour, sex or culture, we are all living our 21 day challenge, for whom we wish to be remembered, so go and live out your life as you wish it to be without fear of retribution from misunderstanding from thee.

Not all need to understand as that is everyone's choice, so remember next time the term "Everyone" is used, that this doesn't necessary includes the world as not everyone has a choice.

When I first started this writing competition, it was going to be a collection of philosophical quotes of time past to show an essence of the person whom I am, but as in life, circumstances change the course of our destiny to be as unique as we are with our features and fingerprints.

We live our lives within this one planet with a few individuals whom get to leave the boundaries into outer space, to show us the marvels beyond everyone else's reach. The word "everyone" is used as simple as we use water when having a shower or bath without the consideration that not everyone is as privileged.

If everyone is everyone as when the word is used so widely to include everyone on the one planet which everyone actually shares and lives upon, why is it that everyone is not getting the same privileges as each other to live a life of happiness and prosperity?

The answer to that question is as unique as we
are in how we live our lives from day to day
which my 21 day writing challenge will
hopefully portray, from the start where with one
of my own original poems put onto a site for
poetry to this one which reflects my personality.